NORTHWEST
Passages

NORTHWEST

from the pen of
JOHN MUIR

In California, Oregon, Washington, and Alaska

Introduction by Scott Lankford
Designed and Illustrated by Andrea Hendrick

Tioga Publishing Company
Palo Alto, California

COPYRIGHT ©1988, Tioga Publishing Co., P.O. Box 50490,
Palo Alto, CA 94303
Art copyright ©1988, Andrea Hendrick   *First Printing*

Northwest Passages features selections from the following
works by John Muir:

> *Picturesque California* (1888)
> *The Mountains of California* (1894)
> *Our National Parks* (1901)
> *Travels in Alaska* (1915)
> *Steep Trails* (1918)

From STEEP TRAILS by John Muir. Copyright 1918 by
Houghton Mifflin Company. Copyright renewed 1946 by
Helen Muir Funk. Reprinted by permission of Houghton
Mifflin Company.

From JOHN OF THE MOUNTAINS: UNPUBLISHED
JOURNALS OF JOHN MUIR edited by Linnie Marsh Wolfe.
Copyright 1938 by Wanda Muir Hanna. Copyright ©
renewed 1966 by John Muir Hanna and Ralph Eugene Wolfe.
Reprinted by permission of Houghton Mifflin Company.

LIBRARY OF CONGRESS
Library of Congress Cataloging-in-Publication Data

Muir, John 1838-1914.
   Northwest passages: from the pen of John Muir in
California, Oregon, Washington, and Alaska /
introduction by Scott Lankford; designed and illustrated
by Andrea Hendrick.
      p.   cm.

   ISBN 0-935382-66-6 :
   1. Muir, John, 1818-1914.   2. Natural history—
Northwest, Pacific.   3. Natural history—Alaska.
4. Conservationists—United States—Biography.
5. Naturalists—United States—Biography.
I. Lankford, Scott, 1957-   . II. Title.
QH31.M9A3 1988a
508.79—dc19   88-12316
                                                  CIP

INTRODUCTION

JOHN MUIR'S NORTHWEST PASSAGE

John Muir, America's most celebrated natural-ist and conservationist, made his last great jour-ney through the wilderness of the Pacific Northwest over one hundred years ago, in 1888. In a life filled to overflowing with wilderness wanderings, this may be the most important passage of them all. Burdened by the cares of a growing family and the administration of his father-in-law's orchards in Martinez, California, Muir had been far too busy to visit the mountain wilderness of the West (his spiritual home) for almost seven years. "I'm a horrible example," he confessed to an old climbing companion. "I, who have breathed the mountain air – who have really lived a life of freedom – condemned to penal servitude with these miserable little bald-heads! [holding up a bunch of cherries]. Boxing them up; putting them in prison! And for money! Man! I'm like to die of the shame of it."[1]

Once the most famous nature writer in America, Muir could no longer find the time to write about the mountains. "We fear that you may have abandoned literature altogether . . ." wrote his bewildered editors. "Has the ink in your fountain entirely dried up?"[2] Even Muir's physical health, once indestructible, seemed increasingly fragile. At age fifty he described himself as "all nerve-shaken and lean as a crow — loaded with care, work, and worry."[3]

Could this possibly be the same man who, twenty years before, had walked a thousand miles on foot from Wisconsin to Florida just for the adventure of it? The pioneering mountaineer who had accomplished the first ascent of Mount Ritter and dozens of other High Sierra peaks? The dedicated naturalist who spent weeks and months tramping through Yosemite with little more than bread and a blanket to sustain him?

Finally in 1888, near desperation, Muir's wife Louie literally ordered him out of the house, packing him off on a long wilderness journey of several months. Accompanied by the famous botanist Charles Parry, Muir first journeyed east to Lake Tahoe then north past the volcanic peaks of Shasta, Hood, Rainier, and on to Alaska. Spiritually as well as physically, that journey soon became one of the great turning points in Muir's long and eventful life — a Northwest Passage, a watershed divide between two careers, two philosophies, two ways of life.

At first Muir was far too sick and "nerve-shaken" to enjoy traveling at all. He missed his wife, his children (his "bairns" as he called them), and still felt haunted by practical and financial problems back at the ranch. Even his travel journals (from which many of the quotations in this collection were taken) seemed at first strangely empty, with little hint of the torrent of words soon to come.

There were other, far more serious, problems to be confronted. What Muir saw around him as he journeyed toward Lake Tahoe appalled him. The Sierra Nevada wilderness he had loved and written about as a younger man seemed now perilously close to destruction: the forests logged from valley floor to timberline, the streams and lakes muddy with eroded topsoil, and the once-flourishing mountain meadows gnawed and trampled into dust by multitudes of domestic sheep — "hooved locusts" as Muir once bitterly described them. By 1888 the ecological health of the California mountains seemed almost as broken and barren as Muir's own personal sense of well-being.

Fortunately, as Muir turned north toward Mount Shasta and beyond, both his health and his spirits began to improve. So did the landscape. Sheltered from the exploitive onrush of the California gold rush and its aftermath, the wilderness of the Pacific Northwest remained, by comparison, relatively unspoiled. Muir felt immensely cheered by the sight of it. On a northbound train he wrote to his wife that he would soon "be well at Shasta beneath a pine tree."[4] Yet still the old cares plagued him. Should he not cut his trip short and return home to help with the ranch?

His wife's letter in reply surely counts as among the most eloquent Muir ever received. In a sense, Muir's career as America's foremost conservationist, the father of the National Park and Forest System, the founder of the Sierra Club, the camping companion of presidents Roosevelt and Taft, all date from the moment in 1888 when he first broke the seal on that extraordinary letter.

> A ranch that needs and takes the sacrifice of a noble life ought to be flung away beyond all reach and power for harm . . . The Alaska book and the Yosemite book, dear John, must be written, and you need to be your own self, well and strong, to make them worthy of you. There is nothing that has a right to be considered beside this except the welfare of our children.[5]

Having freed (or forced) her ailing husband to travel, to leave the cares of the everyday world behind, she now freed (or forced) him to become an author once more. Family cares were of secondary importance. All that mattered was Muir's health, and the health of his writing. It was, his wife realized, the work that her husband had been born to do (here it may truly be said that she knew her husband better than he knew himself).

Encouraged by Louie's letter, Muir did indeed begin writing again. And climbing. Surprised by joy, he was soon clambering to the summit like a youngster — and penning his famous account of an "Ascent of Mount Rainier" along the way. "Did not mean to climb it," he bragged to his wife exultantly, "but got excited and was soon on the top!"[6] The climb of Rainier might well be taken as a metaphor for Muir's Northwest Passage as a whole. Climbing up out of the despair which at times had nearly engulfed him, by the end of his journey he was, as his wife Louie had predicted, finally his "own self" again, "well and strong."

Continuing north, Muir was also astonished and deeply moved by the magnificent landscape of the Pacific Northwest he saw spread out before him. True, he had journeyed through the same region twice before: once in 1879, shortly after proposing marriage to Louie; and again in 1880, shortly after marrying her. But never before had the boundless beauty and bounty of the Pacific Northwest so overwhelmed him as now. Even Yosemite and the High Sierra, his old favorites, seemed pale by comparison. Humbled by the sight of an Alaskan sunrise, he wrote,

> I never before had the scenery before me
> so hopelessly, over-abundantly beautiful for
> description . . . Even one's first view of the
> High Sierra after climbing from height to
> height through the veiled woods . . . may be

attempted, and some kind of description,
some picture more or less telling, made of
them . . . But here it is so nearly endless . . .
so tender, so fine, so ethereal, any penwork
seems coarse and utterly unavailing.[7]

Part of Muir's personal enthusiasm for the
wilderness landscape of the Pacific Northwest
was, of course, just that: purely personal. Far from
home, his health returning, he felt a flood of
physical and spiritual good feeling that might have
brightened any landscape on earth. But much of
Muir's enthusiasm was also based on the harsh
historical contrast — plainly visible in stark
economic, political, and ecological terms —
between the relatively untouched wilderness of
the Pacific Northwest and the already vanishing
wilderness of California. Metaphorically speaking,
Muir's Northwest Passage was also a journey back-
ward through time. Back to a place and an era in
which vast tracts of the American wilderness
remained largely unexplored and unexploited.

Thus mile by mile, mountain by mountain, the
landscape of the Pacific Northwest gradually took
on a whole new political (even metaphysical) sig-
nificance for Muir. By the time he reached Alaska
a new personal and political philosophy had
begun to take shape in his mind — one that
would eventually transform both John Muir and
the nature of America together. A portion of this
magnificent wilderness might, he concluded,

be set apart and protected for public use forever, containing at least a few hundreds of these noble pines, spruces, and firs. Happy will be the men, who, having the power and the love and the benevolent forecast to do this, will do it. They will not be forgotten. The trees and their lovers will sing their praises, and generations yet unborn will rise up and call them blessed.[8]

This is, of course, precisely the ideal for which Muir remains most famous today: the notion of an interlocking system of national forests and parks, conserving both the wealth and the wonders of the American wilderness for the benefit of generations to come. Within a year he was once again flooding the national press with eloquent articles about the western wilderness, just as he had done a decade before, but this time with a difference: for this time Muir spoke not just as a curious naturalist, but as the leader of a national conservation movement.

The glad fact that, over one century later, so much of the magnificent landscape that Muir described still remains intact is eloquent testimony to his his success, as both an artist and a politician. More than any other American, Muir's personal philosophy has literally been etched onto the landscape, both in those parks and preserves for which he fought directly (such as Mount Rainier National Park) and in the dozens of other national, state, and local wilderness parks whose

creation his writings inspired. It is an extraordinary legacy for any one man, any one
movement, any one generation to have left
behind — an inheritance well worth studying;
an inheritance well worth fighting to protect.

Scott Lankford
Stanford University, 1988

[1] Frederick Turner, *Rediscovering America: John Muir In His Time and Ours* (Viking: New York, 1985), pp. 272-3.

[2] Robert Underwood Johnson, Muir's editor at the *Century* Magazine, quoted in Stephen Fox, *The American Conservation Movement: John Muir and His Legacy* (Wisconsin: The University of Wisconsin Press, 1981), pp. 86-7.

[3] William Frederick Bade, *The Life and Letters of John Muir* (Boston: Houghton Mifflin Co., 1918), pp. 218-9.

[4] William Frederick Bade, *The Life and Letters of John Muir* (Boston: Houghton Mifflin Co., 1918), p. 219.

[5] Linnie Marsh Wolfe, *John of the Mountains: The Unpublished Journals of John Muir* (Wisconsin: The University of Wisconsin Press, 1979), p. 282.

[6] William Frederick Bade, *The Life and Letters of John Muir* (Boston: Houghton Mifflin Co., 1918), pp. 215-6.

[7] Linnie Marsh Wolfe, *John of the Mountains: The Unpublished Journals of John Muir* (Wisconsin: The University of Wisconsin Press, 1979), pp. 248-9.

[8] Frederick Turner, *Rediscovering America: John Muir In His Time and Ours* (Viking: New York, 1985), p. 275.

. . . going out I found that I was really
going in.

California

No pain here, no dull empty hours,
   no fear of the past
   no fear of the future . . .
Drinking this champagne water
   is pure leisure,
so is breathing the living air . . .

I am always
glad to
touch
the living rock
again
and dip my head
in the high mountain sky.

. . . plain, sky, and mountains ray beauty which you feel. You bathe in these spirit-beams, turning round and round, as if warming at a camp-fire. Presently you lose consciousness of your own separate existence: you blend with the landscape, and become part and parcel of nature.

If my soul could get away from this so-called prison . . . I should hover over the beauty of our own good star. I should study Nature's laws in all their crossings and unions . . . But my first journey would be into the inner substance of flowers.

The mountain winds, like the dew and rain, sunshine and snow, are measured and bestowed with love on the forests to develop their strength and beauty. However restricted the scope of other forest influences, that of the winds is universal. The snow bends and trims the upper forests every winter, the lightning strikes a single tree here and there, while avalanches mow down thousands at a swoop as a gardener trims out a bed of flowers. But the winds go to every tree, fingering every leaf and branch and furrowed bole; not one is forgotten; the mountain pine towering with outstretched arms on the rugged buttresses of the icy peaks, the lowliest and most retiring tenant of the dells; they seek and find them all, caressing them tenderly, bending them in lusty exercise, stimulating their growth, plucking off a leaf or limb as required, or removing an entire tree or grove, now whispering and cooing through the branches like a sleepy child, now roaring like the ocean; the winds blessing the forests, the forests the winds, with ineffable beauty and harmony as the sure result.

Glaciers
move
in
tides.

So
do
mountains.

So do all things.

Storms are fine speakers, and tell all they know, but their voices of lightning, torrent, and rushing wind are much less numerous than the nameless still, small voices too low for human ears; and because we are poor listeners we fail to catch much that is fairly within reach. Yet we may draw enjoyment from storm sounds that are beyond hearing, and storm movements we cannot see. The sublime whirl of planets around their suns is as silent as raindrops oozing in the dark among the roots of plants.

All things were warming and awakening. Frozen rills began to flow, the marmots came out of their nests in boulder piles and climbed sunny rocks to bask, and the dun-headed sparrows were flitting about seeking their breakfasts. The lakes seen from every ridge-top were brilliantly rippled and spangled, shimmering like the thickets of the low dwarf pines. The rocks, too, seemed responsive to the vital heat — rock crystals and snow crystals thrilling alike. I strode on exhilarated, as if never more to feel fatigue, limbs moving of themselves, every sense unfolding like the thawing flowers, to take part in the new day harmony.

These beautiful days must enrich all my life. They do not exist as mere pictures — maps hung upon the walls of memory — but they saturate themselves into every part of the body — and live always.

Now came the solemn, silent evening.
Long, blue, spiky shadows crept out across
the snow-fields, while a rosy glow, at first
scarce discernible, gradually deepened and
suffused every mountain top, flushing the
glaciers and the harsh crags above them.
This was the alpenglow, to me one of the
most impressive of all the terrestrial
manifestations of God . . . Just before the
alpenglow began to fade, two crimson
clouds came streaming across the summit
like wings of flame, rendering the sublime
scene yet more impressive; then came
darkness and the stars.

. . . the lake was fairly blooming in the
purple light, and was so responsive to the
sky in both calmness and color it seemed
itself a sky. No mountain shore hides its
loveliness. It lies wide open for many a
mile, veiled in no mystery but the
mystery of light.

Tracing rivers to their fountains makes the most charming of travels. As the life-blood of the landscapes, the best of the wilderness comes to their banks, and not one dull passage is found in all their eventful histories.

How many caves and fountains that no eye has yet seen lie with all their fine furniture deep down in the darkness, and how many shy wild creatures are at home beneath the grateful lights and shadows of the woods, rejoicing in their fullness of perfect life.

The deeps of the sky are mottled with singing wings of every color and tone — clouds of brilliant chrysididae dancing and swirling in joyous rhythm, golden-barred vespidae, butterflies, grating cicadas and jolly rattling grasshoppers — fairly enameling the light, and shaking all the air into music.

Thus, by forces seemingly antagonistic and destructive, Nature accomplishes her beneficent designs — now a flood of fire, now a flood of ice, now a flood of water; and again in the fullness of time an outburst of organic life — forest and garden, with all their wealth of fruit and flowers, the air stirred into one universal hum with rejoicing insects, a milky way of wings and petals, girdling the new-born mountain like a cloud, as if the vivifying sunbeams beating against its sides had broken into a foam of plant-bloom and bees.

Oregon

So truly blind is
lord man; so pathetically
employed in his little jobs of
town-building, church-building,
bread-getting, the study of the
spirits and the heavens, that he
can see nothing of the heaven
he is in.

he waves from the deep Pacific, driven by the gale, broke in a grand display of foam on these bald, hardy islets, leaping over them, at a height of a hundred feet perhaps, in magnificent curving sheets, jagged-edged and flame-shaped, draping the rocks with graceful folds of foam-lace from top to bottom, through the meshes of which the black rock showed in striding contrast, and brought the white lacework ever wasting, ever renewed, into relief. I gazed enchanted as long as they were in sight, watching the exultant, triumphant gestures of the tireless breaking waves, and the explosive upspringing and gentle overarching of the white, purple-tinged foam and spray, sifted with sunshine and fashioned by the wind. How calm and peaceful and graceful they were, combined with tremendous displays of power! — a truly glorious show, however common, and a glorious song.

No American
wilderness that I know of is so
dangerous as a city home "with
all the modern improvements."
One should go to the woods
for safety, if for nothing else.

Nevertheless, the countless hosts waving at home beneath their own sky, beside their own noble rivers and mountains, and standing on a flower-enameled carpet of mosses thousands of square miles in extent, attract but little attention. Most travelers content themselves with what they chance to see from car windows, hotel verandas, or the deck of a steamer on the lower Columbia — clinging to the battered highways like drowning sailors to a life-raft . . . all sorts of exaggerated or imaginary dangers are conjured up, filling the kindly, soothing wilderness with colds, fevers, Indians, bears, snakes, bugs, impassable rivers, and jungles of brush to which is always added quick and sure starvation.

On the highest
mountains of the
Cascade Range
the WILD GOAT roams in comparative
security, few of his enemies caring to
go so far in pursuit and to hunt on
ground so high and so dangerous. He is a
brave, sturdy, shaggy mountaineer of an
animal, enjoying the freedom and
security of crumbling ridges and
overhanging cliffs above the glaciers . . .
They seem to be as much at home on the
ice and snow-fields as on the crags,
making their way in flocks from ridge to
ridge on the great volcanic mountains by
crossing the glaciers that lie between
them, traveling in single file guided by an
old experienced leader, like a party of
climbers on the Alps.

There are wonderful ferneries about the misty waterfalls, some of the fronds ten feet high, others the most delicate of their tribe, the maidenhair fringing the rocks within reach of the lightest dust of the spray, while the shading trees on the cliffs above them, leaning over, look like eager listeners anxious to catch every tone of the restless waters.

No lover of trees
will ever forget his
first meeting with
the Sugar Pine.

The sugar pines are as free
from conventional forms as any of the
oaks. No two are so much alike as to hide
their individuality from any observer. Every
tree is appreciated as a study in itself . . .
The branches, mostly near the summit are
sometimes nearly forty feet long, feathered
richly all around with short, leafy branchlets,
and tasselled with cones a foot and a half long.
And when these superb arms are outspread,
radiating in every direction, an immense crown-
like mass is formed which, poised on the noble
shaft and filled with sunshine, is one of the
grandest forest objects conceivable. But though
so wild and unconventional when full-grown,
the sugar pine is a remarkably regular tree in
youth, a strict follower of coniferous fashions,
slim, erect, tapering, symmetrical, every branch
in place. At the age of fifty or sixty years this
shy, fashionable form begins to give way.
Special branches are thrust away from the
general outlines of the trees and bent down
with cones. Henceforth it becomes more and
more original and independent in style, pushes
boldly aloft into the winds and sunshine,
growing ever more stately and beautiful, a joy
and inspiration to every beholder.

Any fool can destroy trees. They cannot run away; and if they could, they would still be destroyed — chased and hunted down as long as fun or a dollar could be got out of their bark hides, branching horns, or magnificent bole backbones. Few that fell trees plant them; nor would planting avail much towards getting back anything like the noble primeval forests. During a man's life only saplings can be grown, in the place of the old trees — tens of centuries old — that have been destroyed. It took more than three thousand years to make some of the trees in these Western woods, trees that are still standing in perfect strength and beauty, waving and singing in the mighty forests . . . Through all the wonderful, eventful centuries since Christ's time — and long before that — God has cared for these trees, saved them from drought, disease, avalanches, and a thousand straining, leveling tempests and floods; but he cannot save them from fools . . .

Thousands of tired, nerve-shaken, over-
civilized people are beginning to find out that
going home to the mountains is going home;
that wildness is a necessity; and that
mountain parks and reservations are useful
not only as fountains of timber and
irrigating rivers, but as fountains of life.
Awakening from the stupefying effects of the
vice of over-industry and the deadly apathy of
luxury, they are trying as best they can to
mix and enrich their own little ongoings with
those of nature, and to get rid of rust and
disease. Briskly venturing and roaming, some
are washing off sins and cobweb cares of the
devil's spinning in all-day storms on
mountains; sauntering in resiny pinewoods or
in gentian meadows, brushing through
chaparral, bending down and parting sweet,
flowery sprays; tracing rivers to their sources,
getting in touch with the nerves of Mother
Earth; jumping from rock
to rock, feeling the souls
of them, panting in the
whole-souled exercise,
and rejoicing in deep,
long-drawn breaths of
pure wildness.

Washington

. . . when at last the whole sky is clear
the colossal cone of Mount Rainier may
be seen in spotless white, looking down
over the dark woods from a distance of
fifty or sixty miles, but so high and
massive and so sharply outlined, it seems
to be just back of a strip of woods only a
few miles wide.

Of all the fire-mountains which, like beacons, once blazed along the Pacific Coast, Mount Rainier is the noblest in form, has the most interesting forest cover, and, with perhaps the exception of Shasta, is the highest and most flowery. Its massive white dome rises out of its forests, like a world by itself, to a height of fourteen thousand to fifteen thousand feet. The forests reach to a height of a little over six thousand feet, and above the forests there is a zone of the loveliest flowers, fifty miles in circuit and nearly two miles wide, so closely planted and luxuriant that it seems as if Nature, glad to make an open space between woods so dense and ice so deep, were economizing the precious ground, and trying to see how many of her darlings she can get together in one mountain wreath . . .

The woods arise in shaggy majesty, every light giving tints of exquisite softness to all the wilderness. Trees ancient-looking abound in damp gullies and on stream-banks, forming the forest primeval . . . Here are true Gothic temples with tree-shafts pointed and aspiring.

When one is
alone at night
in the depths of these woods,
the stillness is at once awful
and sublime.

Every leaf seems to speak.
One gets close to Nature, and
the love of beauty grows as it
cannot in the distractions of a
camp. The sense of utter
loneliness is heightened by
the invisibility of bird or beast
that dwells here . . .

But it is not in the deeps of the woods that people are soothed into perfect rest, nor in mountain valleys, however beautifully bounded by lofty walls. One feels submerged and ever seeks the free expanse. Nor yet on lofty summits, islands of the sky, but on the tranquil uplands where exhilarating air and a free far outlook are combined with the loveliest of the flora. In that zone below the ice and snow and above the darkling woods, where the sunshine sleeps on alpine gardens and the young rivers flow rejoicing from the glacial caves, and the groves of eriogonums are open to the light — perfect quietude is there, and freedom from every curable care.

*A*n Ascent of Mount Rainier

I n all excursions, when danger is realized, thought is quickened, common care buried, and pictures of wild, immortal beauty are pressed into the memory, to dwell forever.

In climbing where the danger is great, all attention has to be given the ground step by step, leaving nothing for beauty by the way. But this care, so keenly and narrowly concentrated, is not without advantages. One is thoroughly aroused. Compared with the alertness of the senses and corresponding precision and power of the muscles on such occasions, one may be said to sleep all the rest of the year. The mind and body remain awake for some time after the dangerous ground is passed, so that arriving on the summit with the grand outlook — all the world spread below — one is able to see it better, and bring to the feast a far keener vision, and reaps richer harvests than would have been possible ere the presence of danger summoned him to life. Danger increasing is met with increasing power, and when thus successfully met, produces an exalted exhilaration joined with an increase of power over every muscle far beyond the experience possible in flat lowlands, where hidden dangers destroy without calling forth any strength to resist or enjoy.

At length, after gaining the upper extreme of our guiding ridge, we found a good place to rest and prepare ourselves to scale the dangerous upper curves of the dome. The surface almost everywhere was bare, hard, snowless ice, extremely slippery, and though smooth in general, it was interrupted by a network of yawning crevasses, outspread like lines of defense against any attempt to win the summit. Here every one of the party took off his shoes and drove steel caulks about half an inch long into them, having brought tools along for the purpose, and not having made use of them until now so that the points might not get dulled on the rocks ere the smooth, dangerous ice was reached. Besides being well shod, each carried an alpenstock, and for special difficulties we had a hundred feet of rope and an axe.

Thus prepared, we stepped forth afresh, slowly groping our way through tangled lines of crevasses, crossing on snow bridges here and there after cautiously testing them, jumping at narrow places, or crawling around the ends of the largest, bracing well at every point with our alpenstocks and setting our spiked shoes squarely down on the dangerous slopes. It was nerve-trying work, most of it, but we made good speed nevertheless, and by noon all stood together on the summit, save one who, his strength failing for a time, came up later.

We remained on the summit nearly two hours, looking about us at the vast maplike views, comprehending hundreds of miles of the Cascade Range, with their black interminable forests and white volcanic cones in glorious array reaching far into Oregon; the Sound region also, and the great plains of eastern Washington, hazy and vague in the distance.

Clouds began to gather. Soon of all the land only the summits of the mountains, St. Helen's, Adams, and Hood, were left in sight, forming islands in the sky.

Alaska

Everybody needs beauty as well as
bread, places to play in and pray
in where Nature may heal and
cheer and give strength to body
and soul alike.

This is one of the still, hushed, ripe days when we fancy we might hear the  beating of nature's heart.

There is a love of
wild Nature
in everybody,
an ancient
mother-love
ever showing
itself whether
recognized or no,
and however
covered by cares
and duties.

. . . The wilderness, I believe, is
dear to every man though
some are afraid of it. People
load themselves with
unnecessary fears, as if there
were nothing in the wilderness
but snakes and bears who, like
the Devil, are going restlessly
about seeking whom they may
devour. The few creatures
there are really mind their own
business, and rather shun
humans as their greatest
enemies. But men are like
children afraid of their mother,
like the man who, going out
on a mist morning, saw a
monster who proved to be his
own brother.

The clearest way
into the Universe
is through a
forest wilderness.

I never saw a disconcerted tree.

They grip the ground as though they

liked it, and though fast rooted they travel
about as we do. They go wandering forth
in all directions with every wind, going
and coming like ourselves, traveling with
us around the sun two million miles a day.

Pollution, defilement,
squalor are words that
never would have been
created had man lived
conformably to Nature.
Birds, insects, bears die as
cleanly and are disposed of
as beautifully as flies. The
woods are full of dead and
dying trees, yet needed for
their beauty to complete
the beauty of the living . . .

The living

and dead
look well
together
in woods.
Trees
receive a most
beautiful burial.
Nature takes fallen trees gently to
her bosom — at rest from storms.
They seem to have been called
home out of the sky to sleep now.

Rounded masses of hard, resisting rocks rise everywhere along the shore and in the woods, their scored and polished surfaces still unwasted, telling of a time, so lately gone, when the whole region lay in darkness beneath an all-embracing mantle of ice.

Most people are *on* the world,
not in it — have no conscious sympathy
or relationship
to anything
about them —

undiffused,

separate,

and rigidly
alone like marbles of polished stone,
touching but separate.

In
the mountains,
free, unimpeded,
the imagination feeds
on objects immense and eternal.
Divine influences,
however invisible,
are showered down on us
as thick as snowflakes.

I set out to climb a mountain for comprehensive views; and before I had reached a height of a thousand feet the rain ceased, and the clouds began to rise from the lower altitudes, slowly lifting their white skirts, and lingering in majestic, wing-shaped masses about the mountains that rise out of the broad, icy sea. These were the highest and whitest of all the white mountains, and the greatest of all the glaciers I had yet seen. Climbing higher for a still broader outlook, I made notes and sketched, improving the precious time while sunshine streamed through the luminous fringes of the clouds, and fell on the green waters of the fiord, the glittering bergs, the crystal bluffs of the two vast glaciers, the intensely white, far-spreading fields of ice, and the ineffably chaste and spiritual heights . . . which were now hidden, now partly revealed, the whole making a picture of icy wildness unspeakably pure and sublime.

The mountains are fountains of
men as well as of rivers, of
glaciers, of fertile soil . . .
silent, inaudible, invisible
flow. The very mountains
flowing to the sea. The great
heart of the hills sending its
life down in streams . . .
among the stems and
beneath the leaves of the
lilies . . . Mountains die that
we may live.

When I look on a glacier, I see the immeasurable sunbeams pouring faithfully on the outspread oceans, and the streaming uprising vapors entering cool mountain basins and taking their places in the divinely beautiful six-rayed daisies of snow that go sifting, glinting to their appointed places on the sky-piercing mountains, joining ray to ray, forming glaciers amid the boom and thunder of avalanches, and at last flowing serenely back to the sea.

To dine with a glacier on a sunny day is a glorious thing and makes common feasts of meat and wine ridiculous. The glacier eats hills and drinks sunbeams.

The very thought of this
. . . glacier garden, is an
exhilaration. Though it is 2500
feet high, the glacier flowed
over its ground as a river flows
over a boulder; and since it
emerged from the icy sea as
from a sepulcher it has been
sorely beaten with storms; but
from all those deadly, crushing,
bitter experiences comes this
delicate life and beauty, to
teach us that what we in our
faithless ignorance and fear call
destruction is creation.

The scenery of the ocean, however sublime in vast expanse, seems far less beautiful to us dry-shod animals than that of the land seen only in comparatively small patches; but when we contemplate the whole globe as one great dewdrop, striped and dotted with continents and islands, flying through space with other stars all singing and shining together as one, the whole universe appears as an infinite storm of beauty.

John Muir
Earth-planet,
Universe

NORTHWEST PASSAGES *is typeset in Andover type by Proteus Typography in Palo Alto, CA. The illustrations and book design are by Andrea Hendrick and the calligraphy is by Jody McMillan. The paper is Ticonderoga 70 lb. text, printed and bound by Arcata Graphics/Kingsport, Tennessee.*

NORTHWEST PASSAGES *is typeset in Andover type by Proteus Typography in Palo Alto, CA. The illustrations and book design are by Andrea Hendrick and the calligraphy is by Jody McMillan. The paper is Ticonderoga 70 lb. text, printed and bound by Arcata Graphics/Kingsport, Tennessee.*